MARTIAL ARTS
HOME TRAINING

MARTIAL ARTS HOME TRAINING

The Complete Guide to the Construction and Use of Home Training Equipment

Mike Young

Tuttle Publishing

Boston • Rutland, VT • Tokyo

First published in 1999 by Tuttle Publishing, with editorial offices at 153 Milk Street, Boston,
Massachusetts 02109.

Library of Congress Cataloging-in-Publication Data

Young, Mike
      Martial arts home training : the complete guide to the
   construction and use of home training equipment / by Mike Young. --
   1st ed.
         p. cm.
      Includes bibliographical references (p.).
      ISBN 0-8048-3170-X (pbk.)
      1. Martial arts--Training. 2 Home gyms--Design and construction.
   I. Title.
   GV1102.7.T7Y68 1997
   796.8--dc21

Distributed by

USA
Tuttle Publishing
Distribution Center
Airport Industrial Park
364 Innovation Drive
North Clarendon, VT 05759-9436
Tel: (802) 773-8930
Tel: (800) 526-2778

CANADA
Raincoast Books
8680 Cambie Street
Vancouver, British Columbia V6P 6M9
Tel: (604) 323-7100
Fax: (604) 323-2600

JAPAN
Tuttle Shokai, Inc.
1-21-13 Seki, Tama Ku
Kawasaki-shi, Kangawa-ken 214
JAPAN
Tel: (81) 44-883-1924
Fax: (810 44-822-0413

SOUTHEAST ASIA
Berkeley Books Pte Ltd
5 Little Road #08-01
Singapore 536983
Tel: (65) 280-1330
Fax: (65) 280-6290

05 04 03 02 01 00 99   10 9 8 7 6 5 4 3 2 1

Printed in the United States of America
Text design by Stephanie Doyle

DEDICATION

This book is dedicated to my parents:

To my late father, Richard K. L. Young, the relentless inventor/junk collector and motivator, who taught me the most valuable lessons in creativity: how to make something useful out of something other people might consider junk. My dad could turn an ordinary piece of wood into a rubber-band gun with a few flicks of his knife. A trip to the local junkyard with my dad was always a hunt for buried treasures.

And to my mother, Elsie S. Young, who always provided me with an encouraging environment: letting me build and create strange and unusual projects around our house at a very young age (and into adulthood). The support of both of my parents was the genesis for this book.

Man's mind stretched to a new idea never goes back to its original dimensions.

—Oliver Wendell Holmes

The only way to discover the limits of the possible is to go beyond them into the impossible.

—Arthur C. Clarke

CONTENTS

ACKNOWLEDGMENTS

I would first like to thank Elsie S. Young, Richard K. L. Young, Margarethe F. Young, Kathy Young, Pat Young, Dean Sensui, Owen Uyehara, Jason Yoshida, Walter Wong, Fred Degerberg, Jim Leone, Ruben Diaz, Mark Wiley, and Randall Roberts, who helped make this book a reality. Without their help, support, guidance, and inspiration, this book would never have been conceived or completed.

There has also been a multitude of martial arts masters and teachers who have been pivotal in my own personal martial arts development, whom I would like to thank. They are listed below in the order in which they came into my life. These people include: Richard Miura (Wado-Ryu Karate), Alfred Dela-Cruz (Chuan-Fa Kajukenbo), Fu-Ling Tung (Tai Chi Chuan), Raymond Tabosa (Escrima), Patrick Hodges (Northern Shaolin, Pa Kua, Hsing-I, and Monkey Kung Fu), Master Hong (Hapkido and Tae Kwon Do), Jason Yoshida (Judo), Eiichi Jumawan (Boxing), Eddy Pedoy (Escrima), Kimo Pang (Internal Shaolin), Hide Hirayama (Taido),

Cherie Jung (Taido), Bob Duggan (Hwa Rang Do), Richard Bustillo (Jeet Kune Do and Kali), Dan Inosanto (JKD and Kali), Randy Duarte (Capoeira), Daniel Duby (Savate), Bernie Pock (Northern Praying Mantis Kung Fu), Walter Wong (Wing Chun), Easie Williams (Boxing), Augusto Franco (Capoeira), Elba Serrano (Capoeira), Andy Lau (Eagle Claw Kung Fu), Bira Almeida (Capoeira), Camisa (Capoeira), Itabora (Capoeira), Fidel Fraijo (Boxing), Al Fraijo (Boxing), Kenny Hui (Northern Shaolin), Richard Sylla (Savate), Fred Degerberg (Eclectic Blend), Lhoucin Benghafour (Savate), Ivan Umek (Savate), Ajarn Surchai (Muay Thai), Francis Fong (Wing Chun), Rorion Gracie (Brazilian Ju-Jitsu), Herman Suwanda (Mande Muda Pencak Silat), Liao Wu Ch'ang (Monkey Boxing), Huang Ken Wang (Shuai Chiao and Sombo), Ken Liu (Pa Kua), Mark Wiley (Kali), Nicholas Saignac (Savate), Bob Koga (Aikido), Machado Brothers (Brazilian Ju-Jitsu), Tony Pascual (Ju-Jitsu), Ron Balicki (Shootwrestling and Kali), Jerry Walker (Lua), Eyal Yanilov (Krav Maga), Hing Piu Ng (Eagle Claw Kung Fu), and Tom Meadows (Combat Whip/Latigo Y Daga).

FOREWORD

In the martial arts—a world steeped in tradition—
revolution is rare. Nonetheless, when it is widely
agreed that a change is for the good of the arts, practitioners embrace it with fervor. One recent revolution was the incorporation of modern training
methodologies. Along with the more familiar training devices, such as China's wooden dummy and
Japan's *makiwara,* came more Westernized workout
gear, such as heavy bags, striking pads, and the simple jump rope. As martial artists became increasing-
ly aware of the need for modern workouts, a primary concern was the cost and availability of the necessary devices. Here is where Mike Young began a revolution of his own. Through his combination of
invention and ingenuity, Mike has helped thousands
of practitioners to develop veritable gyms in their
own backyards. Not only does this save money, but
it provides a connection with the equipment that
ranges from the basic (you can build the equipment
to your height) to the esoteric (some would argue
that building your own equipment is the first medi-
tative step in interacting with it). But regardless of

whether you want to build a classic *dojo* or are just shocked by the cost of a punching bag and want to make your own, Mike has the solution. His instructions are clear, correct, and concise. He recommends materials that are readily available. Best of all, Mike tells you the fastest and best way to build the training tools, so that you can use them as soon as possible and still be using them years from now. It's likely you'll give out before the equipment does. But then, you'll get up the next morning, see this piece of training machinery—complex or simple—that you have built, and once again you'll warm up and work out. Having the proper equipment is inspiring, and Mike Young's knowledge—passed on to you in the following pages—guarantees that in perfecting your martial arts through training, you can start a revolution of your own.

—Marian K. Castinado

Marian K. Castinado is a former executive editor for *World of Martial Arts, Wushu-Kungfu, Dojo, M.A. Training, Karate Kung Fu Illustrated* and *Black Belt Magazine.*

PREFACE

If we all did the things we were capable of doing, we would literally astound ourselves.

—Thomas Edison

After practicing martial arts for many years, I still love training above all of the other aspects that the term "martial arts" may entail.

What I have found over the years is that many martial arts training devices do not fit my specific needs. To practice a technique found only in a certain exotic martial arts system is often difficult without a device specifically designed for that technique.

Enter "Young's Rock & Roll" home training equipment! After years of experimentation and trial and error, I've uncovered the little-known secrets and shortcuts in the construction of personalized home training equipment and will share them in this book. Although this book is just the tip of the iceberg, it's a wake-up call to finding alternative training methods for enhancing one's own martial arts skill!

INTRODUCTION

WHAT'S IN A NAME?

Over the years, many people have tried to put a label on the exact style of martial arts that I teach. I have explored, studied, and practiced many different martial arts for over 30 years. I have always tried to look at the good and bad aspects of different martial arts systems and take the best of what each system had to offer. This is the core theme that martial artists should work for: seek to improve our martial arts skills instead of trying to label a martial arts system or criticize another style. It is the individual martial artist who makes a martial art work, not the martial art itself. Throughout my martial arts career, I have not put much emphasis on naming the system I teach, which is an eclectic blend of the many different martial arts systems.

Through my current profession as a police officer, I have adopted an informal phrase that we used in patrol to name my system. The term often used by my fellow officers when we were about to confront a dangerous situation was "Let's rock and roll." As the years went by, I grew to like this phrase, because just saying those words before a dangerous confrontation seemed to help us relax and perform our job more effectively.

I later coined the term "Young's Rock & Roll" to denote the style that I teach, expressing my way of handling a dangerous confrontation, using whatever method possible to subdue the situation. I like this informal name, because it takes off the rigid edge or seriousness that many martial artists seem to have about the name of their great style. Saying the name "Young's Rock & Roll," one cannot help but smile and wonder what this style is about.

This is what we all need in this world today, a little humor, a little wonder. I joke with my students about the name of our style, continuing with the musical analogy: "it's not classical (traditional martial arts), it's not jazz ("improvised" or untraditional martial arts), it's only Rock & Roll," a simple blend of different martial arts systems trying to play a catchy tune (an effective fighting method). More simply put, it's "martial arts to a different beat!"

"THE FEEL"

Throughout this book, in every chapter, I constantly discuss what I call "the feel." Describing "the feel" is like describing the wind—you know what it is, you know how it feels, but it is very difficult to explain. I will try to give you the best explanation of what I am referring to when I use this terminology.

Whenever I train to develop, maintain, or improve a martial arts technique, I always try to "feel" the proper technique within my body. I believe that the human body has an intrinsic knowledge of proper body mechanics when executing any physical activity, whether it is martial arts or shooting a basketball. No two people will execute the same technique in exactly the same way. There will always be a slight variation because of size, strength, flexibility, coordination, and ability.

This is why the individual must stay in touch with his or her body and be sensitive to its subtle movements and positions, to "feel" the proper technique within the body when a particular physical activity is executed correctly.

Who taught Michael Jordan the proper technique to sink so many baskets consistently in a game? Who taught Muhammad Ali to leave his hands down when boxing or to execute his lightning quick jab? Who taught Bill "Superfoot" Wallace how to kick so flawlessly in competition on one leg? The list goes on and on, but the bottom line is that most stellar athletes listen to their bodies, to how their bodies feel, "how they should be doing it," then they do it so many times that their techniques become flawless and unstoppable. And what techniques are they using? Their own, which have been developed and perfected after countless hours of dedicated practice, or "home training," if you will. Their techniques are not developed only in the gym, at practice, or in the dojo—true technique and training start at home. Home training is what this book is basically about.

So, when training on your martial arts technique at home, strive to feel the proper technique when you execute it correctly. This is why I've always built custom-made home training devices. What feels right for me might not be right for you—the home training device must be specifically designed for you, to accommodate your physical and mental attributes.

Feeling "the feel" or becoming sensitive to "the feel" takes hours and hours of repetitive practice. As your body's muscles, tendons, ligaments, and joints become strengthened and accustomed to the movement, your body will be able to sense whether a technique is being done correctly.

But practicing and feeling what you think is the proper technique is not enough. The technique now must be performed under stressful conditions: competition, the game, sparring, or in combat. This is the empirical test as to whether one's technique works or not. Also, one cannot be discouraged if a technique doesn't work perfectly the first time—this is why we practice.

Once the technique can be utilized correctly under stressful conditions, remember that "feel." Take this "feel" or "frame of mind" back to your home training regimen, and train with that specific mental state. The combination of the two "feelings," the physical skill and the mental state of mind, is the "true feel" one should be striving for when doing home training.

This is *the* feel one should be looking for when one is home training! This I "feel" is true Rock & Roll.

Keep on Rocking!

—Mike Young

Chapter 1

The Need for Training and Testing

I've had a fascination with the martial arts ever since I can remember. Growing up in Hawaii on the island of Oahu, I was constantly exposed to martial arts at a very young age. I can still remember going to Japanese samurai movies when I was four or five years old and dreaming of one day practicing martial arts like "the samurais." At age nine or ten, my friends and I would never miss the Chinese Kung Fu movies that played in several theaters in old downtown Chinatown. We would catch the bus every weekend and savor the experience of a "bloody Kung Fu movie." I would later go home and practice whatever moves I saw in the movie and try to build some of the fascinating Chinese martial arts weaponry.

At a young age, I had already completed making plywood hook-swords, dart-shooting staffs, miniature *shuriken* boomerangs, sword catchers, and many more ingenious devices I saw on the silver screen. The construction of all these devices of destruction was encouraged by my creative dad.

Finally, at age 13, I was allowed to formally study martial arts. I was very excited to start my martial arts training with my father's friend who taught Wado-Ryu Karate a few blocks from my house.

From the first day I started Wado-Ryu Karate, I fell in love with the martial arts. I wanted more, and while living in Hawaii, I studied many martial arts systems, including Cha-3 Kenpo, Tai Chi Chuan, Zen Meditation, Chuan-Fa Kajukenbo, Escrima, Judo, Aikido, Boxing, Kickboxing, Northern and Southern Shaolin, Monkey Boxing, Pa Kua, Hsing-I, Tae Kwon Do, Hapkido, Wing Chun, Internal Shaolin, and whatever I could learn from friends and relatives who studied other martial arts styles.

The beauty of living in Hawaii for me was the wide range of cultures, which brought a rich mixture of martial art traditions, readily available for whoever wanted to practice. Living in the friendly climate of Hawaii, I was always able to train, compete, and exchange ideas with other martial artists from different styles. The Hawaiian environment allowed my martial arts knowledge to expand and let me know that there were a lot of martial arts out in the world to explore.

After reading a magazine article in 1976, I traveled to San Francisco to explore a new martial art from Japan called Taido.

This art woke me up to another dimension in martial arts. When I returned to Hawaii, I continued to train with more enthusiasm, recharged from the recent trip to San Francisco. After tasting new ideas from what islanders call "the mainland," I then attended the legendary Aspen Academy for a month and got exposure to many different martial arts systems.

Returning to Hawaii to work and go to school, I knew I had to go back to the mainland to study all of the other martial arts that were available there. In 1980, after I graduated from the University of Hawaii, I returned to the mainland (Los Angeles) and started to study all the martial arts systems I had read about and now had a chance to study. It was in Los Angeles that I studied Kali, Capoeira, Savate, Tai Mantis, Wrestling, Boxing, Fencing, Wing-Chun, Pencak Silat, Thai Boxing, Gymnastics/Tumbling, Eagle Claw Kung Fu, Judo, Ju-Jitsu, and Shootwrestling, just to name a few! The diverse and eclectic atmosphere of Los Angeles drew martial artists from all over the world to this martial art mecca.

I had adopted the Bruce Lee philosophy of "absorb what is useful" to learn as much as I could about other martial arts and to look for the good and the bad of each martial arts system. I started to cross-train in different systems to develop my own personal fighting style.

A big martial arts reality check came when I became a police officer in 1981 for the Los Angeles County Sheriff's Department. During the police educational process, I quickly found out what did and did not work on the streets. Theory and practice met the streets of L.A., dojo, and home training.

Becoming a police officer further stimulated my martial arts growth because the job exposed me daily to life-and-death situations, situations in which split-second decisions needed to be made regarding whether to use force and, if so, what type and how to use it. I was confronted daily by the lessons of which martial arts techniques did and did not work on the street.

While a police officer, I studied boxing and won more gold medals in boxing than anyone else in the history of the California Police Olympics. Competitive boxing gave me a newfound appreciation for boxers and the rigors they must endure to be on top of their sport! The contact is very real and cardiovascular conditioning is vital, as opposed to the practice and training of many "deadly" martial arts systems.

Fighting for the gold medal in the 1984 California Police Olympics against Wayne Valdez of the LAPD. I won the gold that night.

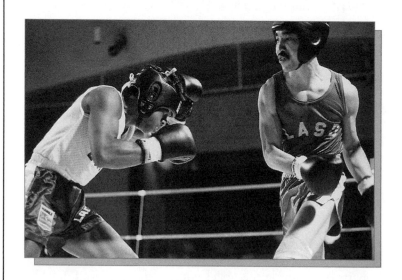

My philosophy is that I will not say I've studied a martial arts system until I have put a great deal of blood, sweat, and tears into the system. Only then can one make an honest evaluation of the system. Then the system must be tested in a free and unrestricted environment where the attacker can strike at you with any type of attack.

San Diego–Los Angeles Sheriff's Department Boxing Team, the "Green Machine," at the California Police Olympics, 1992.

I continue to hold this philosophy to this day. Too many martial artists say they have studied a martial arts system when, in reality, they have only put in a few hours of "sterile" practice. Beware of the charlatans!

CHAPTER 2

DEVELOPING AND MAINTAINING MOTIVATION

My primary motivation for training so hard and developing new and innovative training devices is that practically every week I get out in the middle of the boxing ring and test my martial arts skills against other practitioners in a full-contact setting.

My training philosophy is simple: "If I don't train hard, I will get hit. If I train hard, I won't." My training motivation is even simpler: "I don't like to get hit."

I love the ring because it is in the ring that you can put to the test all the skills that you have been training in for days, weeks, months, or years! The ring also doesn't lie and lull the martial artist into a false sense of security. One will immediately know whether a technique or conditioning routine is working, thanks to the immediate feedback from one's opponent.

I've loved martial arts ever since I can remember and have always been fascinated by how a smaller person could physically overcome a larger person.

Over the years, I've found the age-old philosophy of "practice makes perfect" still holds true to a certain extent, but more important, "*correct* practice makes perfect." Oftentimes, hardcore martial artists will practice one technique over and over in the air, without practicing it against the flesh and developing the proper "feel" of the technique. Without the proper "feel" or "contact" of the practiced technique, a martial artist cannot develop the true feeling of the technique. Consequently, when the incorrectly practiced technique is used in actual fullcontact combat, many times it falls short of the martial artist's expectation.

With this in mind, I have developed much of my own personal home training equipment, along with specific drills to enhance the quality and develop the elusive "feel" of the technique. Many of my home training devices are certainly unique, some never before seen or used in the martial arts world.

From the ring I develop many of my training ideas, always trying to improve on a specific technique, especially when I get hit by a student, or when I cannot land a technique on another martial artist.

From these two primary motivations come all of my ideas for home training equipment and training methods.

Another quirk of my personality is that, because I'm always looking for ways to improve my martial arts technique, I probe many different disciplines that may help me better develop my martial arts abilities—from modern dance to home construction; I try not to restrict my ideas to any specific discipline. Many times when I look at an everyday home item, I wonder how I could use this device in training.

I firmly believe that one can never stop improving unless one chooses not to improve.

I choose to improve forever!

CHAPTER 3

FUNDAMENTALS OF DEVELOPING HOME TRAINING EQUIPMENT

You see things; and you say, "Why?"
I dream things that never were;
and I say, "Why not?"

—George Bernard Shaw

As I've mentioned earlier, my primary motivation for building home training equipment is to develop, practice, and improve "correct" technique, so that it becomes second nature.

I have found that many techniques that I want to practice must be practiced over and over correctly to be perfected. But many times I have no training partner to practice with. Therefore, I build and design most of my training equipment so that the device, most of the time, can be used alone.

I also build many of the home training devices to convey a special "feeling" to me. What I mean by "special feeling" is that the training equipment will have to closely duplicate the "feel" of the actual fighting technique when used in combat.

A good example of developing the "special feeling" is the use of a hanging tire to practice one's Escrima strikes (see Chapter 4). Striking a hard rubber tire with a stick gives me a realistic "feel" of striking a live opponent, because the hanging tire moves unpredictably (like an opponent) and "feels" as solid as a person when it is struck. The hanging tire also gives me the correct "feel" of certain kicks and punches when they are applied properly.

I also like to build home training devices that will enhance a specific martial arts skill and at the same time be fun to work with. When I refer to "fun," I mean that the device will provide me with a gratifying stimulus to eyes, ears, or kinesthetic sense, which will make me want to practice more.

For instance, I use the shadowboxing towel to train the "one-inch-punch." The sound of the snapping of the towel when the punch is executed correctly, the visual stimulus of the towel being jolted by a sudden burst of energy, and the comfortable tactile feel of the fist on the towel actually make practicing the one-inch-punch on the towel fun to do!

Not all of the training equipment I've developed stands alone. The equipment for use with a training partner is intended to simulate the feel of actual fighting conditions, but at the same time makes it fun to train a specific technique.

The "precision blocking stick" is a good example (see Chapter 5). When you practice a specific technique, especially when it involves hitting or blocking, the device emits a loud crack. The quality of the block or strike is known immediately, just by the sound of the crack, which makes it fun to practice.

Some equipment that I construct comes from well-known training devices or methods, but I utilize innovative materials and technology not available a few decades ago. I also try to keep the devices simple to make, so that those who like to work with their hands can easily make most of the devices featured in this book. Although a few devices that I've designed and created require special materials and skills to put together, generally most of my training devices can be made from materials available at any hardware store. The simple acronym KISS (Keep It Simple, Silly) is my primary thought when creating any new piece of training equipment.

Early beginnings of my home training equipment, Hawaii, 1974: spring head dummy, tire dummy, and cement dummy.

Early beginnings of my home training equipment, Hawaii, 1975: early fixed Wing Chun wooden dummy prototype.

Early beginnings of my home training equipment, Hawaii, 1976: balance beam and balance stumps.

Home training with the famous "Rock & Roll" dummy, 1987.

Chapter 4

Tips on Developing a Personal Home Training Routine

Determining one's goals or purpose for practicing martial arts is the key to developing an effective personalized home training routine. Is the practice to develop self-defense skills or coordination, to lose weight, to improve cardiovascular conditioning, to compete in tournaments, to build self-esteem, or confidence?

Once your individual needs are assessed, then a home training routine can be tailored to meet those needs. Therefore, you should determine the purpose for training, then determine and set your goals, then develop the routine/methods to achieve these goals.

Training at home should be part of an overall plan to develop and improve your martial arts skill and should complement and reinforce the techniques taught by a good martial arts instructor. A good instructor can help you develop your home training program and guide you in the right direction to develop the skills needed to be proficient in a particular art. The instructor should also be open to new ideas and training methods, so you do not get too set in specific ways or patterns. (Although many people—especially proud and stubborn martial artists—feel that they don't need an instructor, it is always good to have someone of better skill level than yourself to make sure you are not deviating from the primary focus of developing a specific martial arts skill.)

The home training routine should be carefully tailored to fit the individual's needs in a given amount of time. Determine how much time you have to spend on a workout per week. A general martial arts workout should include stretching, cardio-vascular training, reaction training, general conditioning, strength training, specific skills, and "hands-on" training.

Stretching is vital to any martial artist's workout. Stretching is often neglected in many Western sports-related activities. I especially see this in weight lifters and body builders. These athletes look great but oftentimes cannot even bend over to touch their toes or put their hands behind their backs. In the martial arts, we always want to keep our bodies limber. Neck, shoulders, wrists, back, hips, legs, hamstrings, calves, Achilles tendon, and ankles should all be stretched before starting your workout. The more flexible you are, the less chance there will be of getting injured, and you can also increase the range of motion to a specific joint area to make yourself more versatile and better able to execute specific techniques.

A stretching routine should last for no more than five minutes when you are implementing a complete home training workout. This is not to say that you cannot work out longer to stretch your body, but save time for a specific stretching workout.

Cardiovascular training is basic to martial arts success, health, and longevity. The heart must be trained for at least 20 minutes per workout. Running, StairMaster, Lifecycle, bicycling, and skipping rope are different aerobic exercises you can do to train the cardiovascular system.

Reaction training must be worked on because all techniques, when properly executed, depend on unconscious reaction. Reaction training must be done all the time to eliminate lag time before responding.

General conditioning must also be worked on to develop the strength of large muscle groups and your aerobic capacity. Too many times, martial artists forget this basic rule and wonder why they don't have the strength to keep up with another athlete. General conditioning is the key—basic push-ups, sit-ups, and squat thrusts are examples of general conditioning exercises.

Basic strength-developing exercises should include weight resistance or free weights to strengthen specific muscle groups, as well as a basic bench press routine, squats, curls for the large muscle groups and wrist curls, and shoulder shrugs, etc., for the smaller muscle groups. The fastest way to develop a muscle group is through weight resistance training. At least three sets of 15 repetitions should be done when working a specific muscle group. Once these repetitions can be done comfortably, gradually increase the weight. Many martial artists fail to include a little weight resistance training in their workout routine and wonder why they lack the overall "power" of a specific technique.

Specific skills training is where many of the home training devices I talk about come into play. Maybe one would like to develop a special, angular, powerful right cross. One would spend three to six minutes training the angular right cross on a special piece of equipment that would train this attribute. In this case, one might use the heavy-duty striking post or the shadowboxing towel.

The reason I recommend three to six minutes when working a specialized technique is that one always has to work on proper form, distance, and timing when executing a specific technique. Many times the exact form is crucial to developing the "proper" or correct technique. When doing a technique for only three to six minutes, one's body does not get so tired that the technique becomes sloppy. When the muscles are exhausted by spending too much time on one technique, the technique gets sloppy and the correct technique is not practiced. Only practice specialized skills for a short period of time, then move to another phase of training.

Hands-on training is also essential in home training, but I realize that one is not always going to have a training partner. This is why your time schedule must be exact and specific, so you can arrange time to practice hands-on training at least once a week with a partner, to develop specialized fighting techniques.

So when you design your own home training routine, make sure the above-listed elements are included.

A typical home training routine I would use for maintenance of skills might be something like the following. I would allow myself five hours a week to keep my martial arts skills up to par. I would then allot myself five days of one-hour workouts, which, practically every day, would include:

- First, stretching for 5 minutes
- Reaction training for 10 minutes
- Specific skills training for 3 to 6 minutes
- Cardiovascular training for 20 minutes (usually with a jump rope or in the boxing ring)
- Strength training for 10 minutes
- Then, overall conditioning for the last 6 to 10 minutes, followed by a short cool-down stretching routine

On a day when I could work on the hands-on skills, I would first stretch, then work on hands-on skills for 30 to 40 minutes, then finally work on cardiovascular conditioning.

The reason I work on specialized skills before working on gross muscle or motor skills is that I want my body to be sharp when performing specific and specialized skills. Once I've practiced these skills, the gross motor skills can be worked on for overall general coordination and health.

Remember, your specific home training routine should not be the same as mine. One must take into consideration the time one has to spend on training at home and also specifically what one wants to get out of training martial arts skills at home.

Start home training now! Good luck!

CHAPTER 5

THE SHADOWBOXING TOWEL

During my many years of writing for a popular martial arts magazine about the construction and the use of common and uncommon martial arts training devices, a frequent question readers have asked me is how to make a simple and useful home training device that doesn't involve a lot of special materials.

My response to these readers has been, "Make a shadowboxing towel." I have used a shadowboxing towel for many years but never thought much about it, much less about teaching people how to make one. The usefulness of the shadowboxing towel really hit home one summer when I competed in the California Police Olympics in boxing and Karate. The California Police Olympics is one of the largest diversified athletic events in the country, next to the World Olympic Games.

That summer, I was out to win a sixth consecutive gold medal in boxing and a gold in Karate. I knew the competition would be tough, because people knew who I was and had promised me the year before that they would "destroy" me.

In boxing and Karate, I place the strongest emphasis on conditioning. I also rank raw power (which I feel is developed through hitting the heavy bag) at the top of the list.

That year, one month before the fight, I accidentally cut open the knuckle on my right hand during a camping trip and severely bruised the heel of my foot in sparring. This made hitting the heavy bag almost impossible for me.

I decided to put a greater emphasis on the shadowboxing towel, working with it for a longer period of time. I found that in sparring, my punches were crisper, snappier, and more diversified. I noticed that my footwork was a lot better and that I moved with better balance. Monitoring my pulse rate, I noticed that it also improved by five beats per minute in a week's time.

To make a long story short, I won my sixth consecutive gold medal in boxing and another gold medal in Karate. I attribute a lot of my success to training with the shadowboxing towel.

MATERIALS

The materials you will need to construct the shadowboxing towel are quite simple: a normal bath towel approximately 2 feet × 3 feet will do and a short 6–12-inch piece of masking tape. You may also use a simple 3-inch lag eyehook to hang the towel from (see fig. 1).

CONSTRUCTION

Construction of the shadowboxing towel is very simple. Take your towel and hold it by one corner. Using the tape, attach the towel by the corner where you would hang a heavy bag (see fig. 2). You can also hang the towel from the top frame of a doorway for indoor training (see fig. 3). The towel should be hung at least to your face level, if not lower. The hanging towel will be your target striking area. Tug on the towel gently to see if the tape will hold it in place, and adjust accordingly. To make the hanging of the towel easier, if you are hanging it from a wooden beam or ceiling, insert a lag eyehook into a wooden brace and attach the towel to

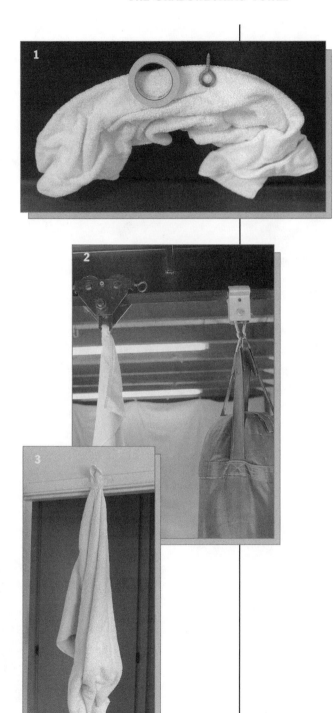

the eyehook (see fig. 4). One now has completed the shadowboxing towel.

TRAINING

While working with the shadowboxing towel, work on focus and snapping your punches and kicks into the towel. Combinations with several consecutive punches and kicks can also be practiced on the towel to give you the feel of follow-through and missing a blow (see fig. 5).

By marking a 3–5 foot distance from the towel, you can practice closing or bridging the gap with your specific style of footwork (see figs. 6 and 7). By imagining the towel as your opponent, you can practice different styles of footwork to evade (see fig. 8) and to attack (see fig. 9) your opponent.

Follow-through and pinpoint accuracy with kicks can be developed by picking a point on the towel (usually at the very tip) and striking it in the appropriate manner. Try kicking five times with one leg (e.g., round-house kick, hook kick, side kick, roundhouse kick, axe kick) to devel-op your balance and pinpoint accuracy (see figs. 10–15).

I have used the shadowboxing towel for many years with remarkable success. It has developed my ability to kick at least six to ten times on one leg with power, without bringing my leg down to the ground. It has also developed my combinations in punching by allowing me to follow through with my combinations in a continuous motion (a heavy bag will stop the follow-through; see fig. 16).

The shadowboxing towel can be an excellent tool to train the accuracy in flying kicks and the more difficult acrobatic kicks (see fig. 17). The resilience of the towel allows you to practice the accuracy and the snap of flying kicks, which are really what makes the flying kick so effective.

The resilience of the towel also allows the practitioner to complete the full range of an acrobatic kick while still working on the accuracy of the kick (see fig. 18). Many times the full range of an acrobatic kick cannot be practiced on a traditional training device (i.e., heavy bag, striking post, kicking shield), because the device will block the full range of the kick.

I have also found the shadowboxing towel to be an excellent tool to develop the short "one-inch" punch of Wing Chun. To do this, put your striking hand approximately one inch away from the towel and snap your vertical fist upward at the towel. The short burst of energy from your fist should

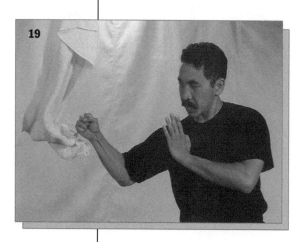

cause the towel to snap sharply forward, allowing you to see the energy transfer from your fist to the towel (see fig. 19). Practicing the one-inch punch on the shadowboxing towel five minutes a day for a few weeks will produce surprising results in the power and snap of your one-inch punch.

This short "jolting," "one-inch" energy is not just confined to the vertical one-inch punch of Wing Chun. The one-inch energy can be practiced with an open palm (see fig. 20), side palm (see fig. 21), or any strike you like to do (see fig. 22). The trick is to explode through the towel 3–5 inches and quickly retract your hand. Eventually try the same strike on a harder object such as a heavy bag, then on your partner. The short, explosive, jolting energy will be felt within a few weeks.

The usefulness of the shadowboxing towel is only limited by your creativity. Try building one and experience the results.

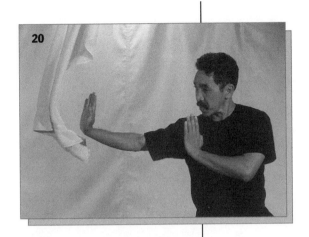

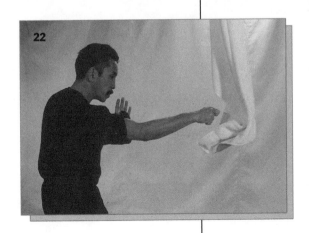

CHAPTER 6

TIRE TRAINING: FOOTWORK, BALANCE, AND LEG DEVELOPER

This chapter and the one following on tire training devices will change the way you look at tires for the rest of your life.

I can remember my fascination with tires from an early age. I remember how I begged my dad not to get rid of an old tire so I could play with it. I liked the durability of the tire and how it would never change its original shape, no matter what I did to it. Eventually, as I got older and started to buy new tires for my own car, I kept the old tires and have created many martial arts training devices that utilize a car or truck tire.

The first training device I'd like to talk about is what I refer to as the "Footwork, Balance, and Leg Developer," also known as an empty tire. I learned about using an empty tire as an excellent training tool a while back while attending an intensive boxing training camp in the San Bernardino Mountains, to sharpen up our team of boxers, whom I regularly train. At the training camp, we utilized a professional boxing gym.

While conducting our usual standard drills of hitting the bags, focus mitts, crazy balls, and sparring, one of the coaches who owned the gym noticed that many of our novice boxers had poor footwork and offered some pointers and advice to help accelerate their learning curve.

Then the main coach, who coached such top professionals as Oscar De la Hoya, Michael Nunn, and Jorge Paez, took out several large truck tires and revealed some little-known trade secrets to help a boxer develop better footwork, balance, and leg strength.

The coach had the boxers stand on the outer edge of the tires as the tires lay flat on the ground. The boxers would then assume a traditional boxing stance, with legs approximately shoulders'-width apart, hands held up, head tucked in. The coach then told the boxers to bounce around the edge of the tires and shadowbox.

As the boxers got used to the rhythm of the movement, the coach would take a regular towel and swing it at the boxers' heads. The boxers' objective was to tuck or weave under the towel to avoid getting hit. As the boxers ducked, they were constantly instructed to look at their opponent, because there is a natural tendency for most novice boxers to look down and not pay attention to incoming blows. After the first two-minute round, our boxers—both novice and advanced—were exhausted! They could barely walk. All of us realized what an excellent training tool the simple tire is.

Keeping the feet balanced over the tire edges forces trainees to spread their feet apart at the proper distance, so they will not cross their feet or put them too close together. This is always a problem among beginning fighters.

The tire immediately became part of the Young's Rock & Roll training devices. I have now utilized the tire for all of the fighters I train, including myself. I've found that using the tire develops the elusive "boxer's balance," which is what I would describe as a "dynamic balance" or "balance in motion."

Many times, martial artists want to demonstrate their "static balance" by standing on one leg and throwing several different kicks without moving, or by holding a low horse stance from which nobody can push them over. This is fine and dandy for demonstration purposes, but for fighting, the balance must be dynamic, always changing. How many boxing, kickboxing, or "anything goes" fights has any individual won by standing still? The tire develops this balance on the move.

All you need, to train with this device, is a simple used thick truck tire. The thicker the tire the better, because the walls of the tire will be supporting your full body weight. Do not use the normal everyday tire you would find on an ordinary automobile, because the walls of those tires are too weak and you will not get the full benefit of the exercise. You can usually get an old discarded truck tire from any high-volume tire dealer-

ship or service station for free.

Once you have the tire, you might want to clean it first, because you will find that fine dust particles and dirt adhere to the sidewall of the tire, and you will get filthy during—and after—a training session.

Use the tire in the manner I mentioned earlier: get into a good boxing stance and move around the outer edge of the tire, moving in both directions, throwing punches at the same time (see fig. 23). Maintain proper balance and don't fall off the edges. Start on the balls of your feet if possible and first start off with from one two-minute round to three three-minute rounds.

As easy as this drill sounds, this exercise is exhausting. Most first-time students cannot do this drill for a full three-minute round without becoming totally exhausted.

As you become more advanced, start throwing a variety of kicks off the tire, which really adds a new dimension to your dynamic balance (see fig. 24). To really keep yourself honest, add a "slip bag" in the path of your head, which will now also work your slipping, bobbing and weaving, balance, footwork, leg strength, and dynamic balance.

A slip bag can easily be made by attaching a small weighted bag to the end of a cord and hanging it at head level (see fig. 25). When you push the bag away, it will come back at your head, simulating a punch. The object of the exercise is to not let the slip bag hit your head, which enhances your ability to "slip" a punch or kick.

The beauty of the tire is that the training device is so simple, so inexpensive (a used tire should not cost a cent), yet so effective. Tire training is now mandatory for all of my fighters when they first start training with me (see fig. 26).

Try working with the phenomenal, high-tech footwork, balance, and leg developer... also known as the tire!

CHAPTER 7

TIRE TRAINING: THE MULTIPURPOSE TIRE

Over years of training, I've found a single empty tire can have a wide array of uses for training yourself in various martial arts systems.

For example, an empty tire hung at about eye level by a thick cord or rope makes an excellent striking target to practice full-power and focused Escrima or Kali strikes with a rattan stick (see fig. 27).

The hanging tire is an excellent striking tool for Escrima for a number of reasons. For one, striking at the hanging tire with a rattan baton feels more realistic than hitting a heavy bag. The hanging tire has unusual edges and angles to strike and to be aware of (like a human body), and it also moves in an unpredictable manner, as a person would in a real fight. I

also enjoy hitting the hanging tire with the stick because I can hit the tire without the fear of destroying an expensive piece of training equipment like a heavy bag, a Wing Chun dummy, or even the Escrima stick itself.

I also lowered the hanging tire to where it barely touched the ground so I could practice low-line attacks with the Escrima sticks (see fig. 28). For added variety, I then hung two tires together, one at head level, the other at leg level, so that I could practice both lines of attack at once. I found the two hanging tires an enjoyable training tool because of the independent movement of both tires at the same time (see fig. 29). This gave me unpredictable and erratic targets to strike at, just as if I were fighting a real live opponent in the street.

A wide variety of Escrima strikes can be practiced. Whipping staccato strikes (see fig. 30), florette strikes (see fig. 31), abiniko strikes (see fig. 32), full-power strikes (see fig. 33), fakes (see figs. 34 and 35), and unusual thrusting strikes (see fig. 36).

I've also found the hanging tire to be an excellent tool to develop strong hand strikes. When the tire is hung at eye, stomach, or leg level, striking the tire with your hand and foot gives you a realistic feel of striking a "real-life" opponent. The unusual angles of the tire, added to the erratic twists and turns of a suspended tire, simulate "real-life" combat situations where your opponent will not be standing still and waiting for a strike. The tire also develops your timing, accuracy, and proper technique, because if you hit the tire at an unusual angle, and your technique is not correct or accurate, you can hurt yourself.

The hanging tire is also an excellent tool for practicing evasive footwork and defensive skills. As I strike the tire, I move away from it, always trying not to let the tire hit me, which lets me dictate when I hit the tire (see fig. 37).

To practice focus and precision in motion, I try to punch into the center of the suspended tire as it is moving. I saw boxers doing this many years ago in an old boxing gym in South Central L.A. The old boxing trainers would swear on this training method to develop focus, precision, and good footwork (see fig. 38).

I also hang the tire low again, at leg level, and practice low-line kicks to the leg and shin area (see fig. 39). I love this exercise because of the solid feel of kicking an object in motion and the unpredictable movement of the hanging tire.

As the tire hangs in the low position, I also practice ground techniques such as ground kicks (see fig. 40), leg locks (see fig. 41), leg traps (see fig. 42), leg breaks (see fig. 43), choking techniques (see fig. 44), and even strengthening the "guard" position (see fig. 45).

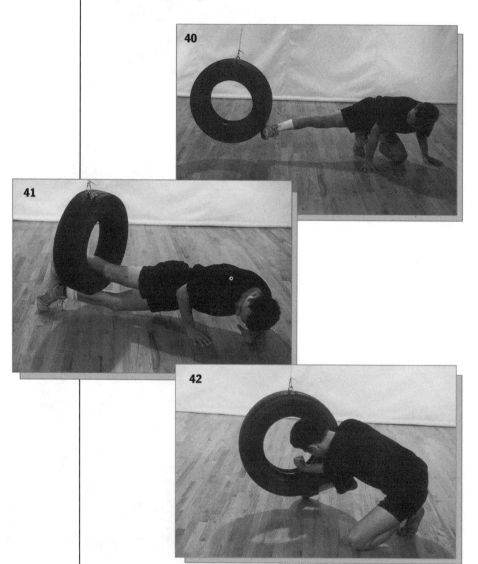

The nice thing about training on the tire is that you can practice your technique with full power, and you don't have to worry about breaking your partner's leg or permanently injuring him or her.

The last training tip utilizing the tire, which all of us martial artists can use, is to develop the explosive power in our legs. This can be done by using the same rope and attached tire.

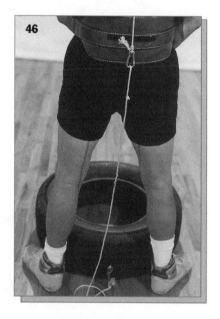

Attach the free end of the rope to the back of a weight belt, then place it around your waist (see fig. 46).

Walk away from the tire approximately 6 to 10 feet, so that the rope is taut (see fig. 47). In a sudden burst, sprint as fast as you can for 40 yards, dragging the tire behind you (see fig. 48). The resistance of the tire dragging on the ground while you sprint develops an explosive burst of power in your legs! Repeat this drill at least five times a workout, sprinting as fast as you can, and watch your explosive power take off. A semipro athlete designed this drill for me after he saw me setting up the hanging tire for my training on a basketball court!

The beauty of tire training is that it doesn't cost you a lot of money to make the device. I just used a heavy-duty tire I got for free at a service station. Drill a 1/4-inch hole in the middle of the tire tread (see fig. 49), then insert a 1/4-inch × 3-inch eyebolt through the hole with the "eye" section placed on the outside of the tire (see fig. 50). Once the eyebolt is inserted, secure it with a 1/4-inch washer and a 1/4-inch nut on the side section of the tire (see fig. 51). When the eyebolt is secure, you can tie a 1/4-inch nylon rope to the eyebolt or attach a fastener clip to the end of the rope (see fig. 52) to hang the tire at the desired height (see fig. 53).

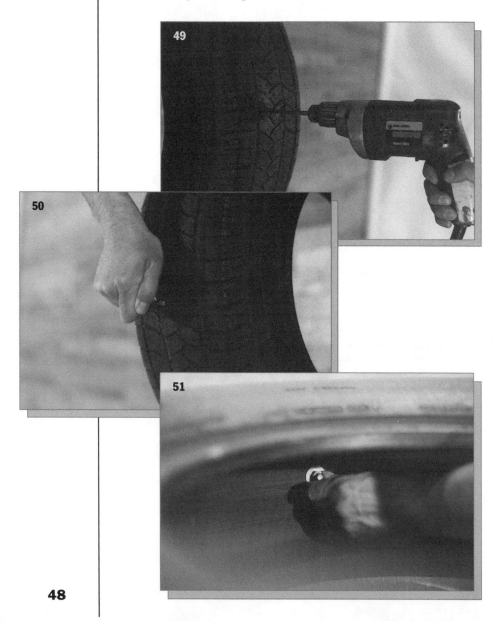

Utilizing the same tire and rope, you can practice developing some explosive power in your legs, doing the outlined drill.

Try building this tire training device—you'll never "tire" of its uses!

CHAPTER 8

THE PRECISION BLOCKING STICK

Many years ago, after not training with my Wing Chun instructor for almost a year, I went back to his house to sharpen up my Wing Chun skills. After several hours of an intensive workout, he brought out a device he said he had been using since I had been away from practice. My instructor claimed that this device had helped his new students develop the precision blocking skills needed to execute effective Wing Chun blocks.

I observed that the device was nothing more than three PVC pipes, duct-taped together, and I wondered how this device could develop the precise movements of the Wing Chun blocks. My instructor then proceeded to demonstrate how he used this simple device to obtain the desired results. First, he had me stand in the Wing Chun "guard," or "ready," position. My instructor then slowly thrust the pipes at me, aiming the tip of the pipes straight at the upper midline of my chest. It was up to me to block the pipes with any Wing Chun block combined with a quick body pivot. After the first block, my instructor told me to hold the blocking position and corrected me on the little intricacies and nuances that make Wing Chun blocks so economical and effective. As my instructor kept thrusting the pipes at me, every time I blocked incorrectly, he would stop and place me in the proper position. I found that the straightness of the pipes added to the proper mechanics of an effective block (see fig. 54).

54

Over 20 minutes elapsed and I was soaking wet from the intensity and precision of this blocking and pivoting exercise. It was clear to me that using this device correctly would great-ly enhance my Wing Chun blocking skills and complement my other martial arts techniques. I have now been using this device for over three years and don't know how I did without it. I affectionately refer to this device as the "precision blocking stick."

To build the device is very easy. All you need is three 39-inch × 1/2-inch schedule 40 PVC tubing, some duct tape, and some rags, and you're all set (see fig. 55). Start building this device by first making sure the three 39-inch PVC pipes are of even length (see fig. 56). Once this is done, grasp all three pipes in one hand and make sure the ends are even with each other.

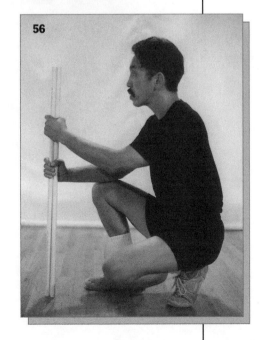

Secure one end of the pipes together with duct tape by wrapping the tape around the circumference of all three pipes. With the three pipes semisecure, pad one end of the pipes with a thick rag and secure the rag to that end with duct tape (the reason for the padded ends is that the sharp edges of the PVC pipes can injure the trainee; see fig. 57). Pad the other end of the pipes in the same fashion. Once this is done, the "precision blocking stick" is complete.

I love this precision blocking stick not only for practicing the technical Wing Chun blocks (see figs. 58–61), but even for the hard Karate (see figs. 62–64) or Kung Fu blocks (see figs. 65 and 66).

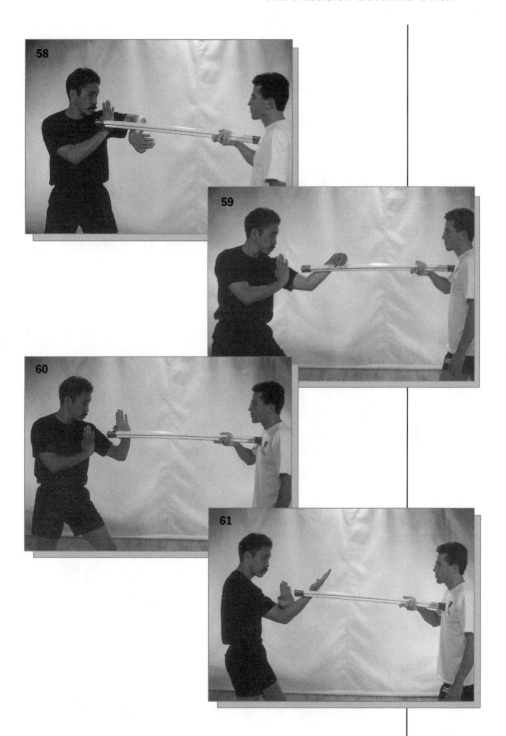

The length of the pipes offers a realistic kicking and blocking angle. The precision blocking stick also helps to condition your forearms (see fig. 67), wrists (see fig. 68), shins (see fig. 69), and insteps (see fig. 70) to a high degree when a partner thrusts or swings the stick at a vital point of your body and you block the stick with the appropriate body part.

Another good reason to use this tool is that, if your training partner's arms or shins are not in condition, he or she can deploy the appropriate strikes (kicks or punches) to you without getting hurt. Many times in hard blocking drills, the training partner has to stop because his or her arms or shins are in so much pain. Using the blocking stick in this way offers another way to practice good blocking skills without injuring your partner. I have used this device for quite a while for blocking and conditioning with excellent results.

The precision blocking stick can also be used to develop
the follow-through in a good roundhouse kick that is often
utilized in Thai Boxing. The basic Thai Boxing method is
kicking bags and pads, which is great, but the bags and pads
fall short because when you kick a bag or pad, you normally
cannot follow through on the kick, thus killing the full range
of motion of the kick.

To develop the follow-through in a kick utilizing the precision blocking stick, have your partner hold one end of the stick at arm's length, away from his or her body, facing you. The other end of the stick should be touching the ground, at a 90-degree angle (see fig. 71). The practitioner should execute a roundhouse kick at the precision blocking stick at exactly where an opponent's thigh would be, approximately 2 inches from the ground (see fig. 72).

When the foot/shin makes contact with the stick (see fig. 73), the foot impacting the stick will make a loud cracking noise if the kick is done correctly. More important, though, is that the kick goes through the full range of motion. The sound and the feel of kicking the stick make you want to practice the roundhouse kick more.

To utilize the precision blocking stick in the Pencak Silat system, more specifically the Harimau, or Ground Tiger, Silat, I use the precision blocking stick as an opponent's leg, to practice the devastating leg breaks and pressure point strikes. The stick is again held by the trainer, perpendicular to the ground (see fig. 74), while the Harimau practitioner practices the sensitive leg locks and takedowns on the precision blocking stick as if it were an opponent's leg (see figs. 75 and 76). I've found this device to be a valuable tool because most people cannot handle the pain of a leg lock or leg pressure point strike. Using the precision blocking stick, practitioners can practice a leg lock or pressure point strike for as long as they want without injuring their training partners.

To improve my grappling skill, I've utilized the precision blocking stick as a grip strengthener. Grabbing the stick with both hands as tightly as possible, squeeze and twist the stick forward and backward 50 times (see figs. 77 and 78). The twisting movement of the PVC pipe is strenuous for the forearms and strengthens one's forearm grip, which is essential in grappling, especially when grappling with a *gi*.

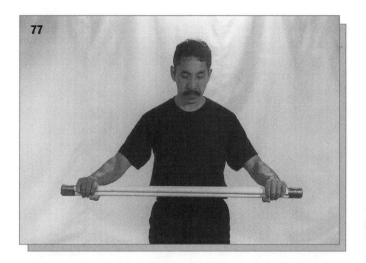

Another grip-strengthening exercise using the precision blocking stick is done by holding on to one end of the stick with one hand while your partner hangs on to the other end of the stick with one hand. The intention of each participant is to pull the stick out of the training partner's hand. This exercise, when done in two-minute rounds, develops the forearm gripping strength to a remarkable degree (see figs. 79 and 80).

With the precision blocking stick, you can also practice a few of the painful arm (see fig. 81) and leg (see fig. 82) locks so common in the grappling arts. Many times, as with the Harimau Silat techniques, you may run out of training partners because of the pain each lock inflicts. The precision blocking stick offers an excellent alternative.

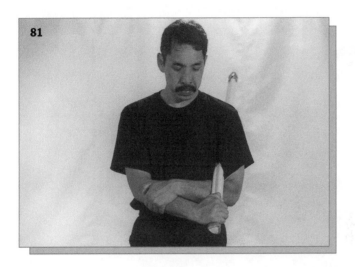

81

82

In the practice of precision knockout kicks of Savate, the trainer holds the stick at one end at an approximately 45-degree angle from the ground (see fig. 83). The Savateur then does a quick, accurate hook kick (called a reverse kick in Savate) to the last 2 inches of the stick (see fig. 84), which should be held at approximately head level. The trainer should then immediately move the stick to a horizontal position, approximately at waist level, and the Savateur should execute

83

84

a quick snappy roundhouse kick to the last 2 inches of the stick, simulating a roundhouse kick to an opponent's solar plexus (see figs. 85–89). The stick should make a loud cracking noise when the kick is executed properly, which is gratifying to hear. I have witnessed many Savateurs go down as a result of this combination, which can be easily learned with the precision blocking stick.

Many of the precision kicks of Savate can be practiced with the stick just by having your training partner hold the stick by one end and striking the last 2 inches of the stick with your shod foot (see figs. 90–92).

The key to success in Savate is speed, accuracy, and snap, which is what the stick can develop.

I also use the precision blocking stick to develop the accurate angle-changing strikes of Escrima. To do this, the trainer holds the middle of the stick with one hand, with his arm almost fully extended and the stick perpendicular to the ground (see fig. 93). The Escrimador should start the motion of one strike aimed at the top of the precision blocking stick, then, approximately 3 to 6 inches before striking the precision blocking stick (see fig. 94), the Escrimador should suddenly change direction and strike the last 2 inches of the bottom of the precision blocking stick (see fig. 95). The trainer should vary the height and the angle of the precision blocking stick periodically to give the Escrimador a sense of fighting a live opponent (see fig. 96). The Escrimador can also strike low first then hit high to give variation of the movements.

Practicing this type of drill with the precision blocking stick develops the Escrimador's ability to fake and change directions on a moment's notice—the same manner in which it is done in combat, in competition, or in the streets.

There are countless drills that can be done with the precision blocking stick to develop different attributes for almost any style. This is why I thoroughly enjoy training with this tool.

It seems that the drills that can be done with this stick are only limited by your own imagination.

CHAPTER 9

THE HEAVY-DUTY STRIKING POST

The *makiwara,* or striking post, has been around for many years, offering a sound and time-tested method for toughening one's hands and feet, but also a way to develop stronger punches and kicks.

The problem I have found in using a makiwara is that the strikes that are usually used on it are straight and linear in nature. This is not to say that ridgehand chops and roundhouse kicks cannot be practiced on it, it's just that you must adjust to a totally different posture to execute the technique. Making the adjustment in posture sometimes leads to the lack of a spontaneous combination of strikes at different levels and angles. Another drawback of the makiwara is that the post is fixed into a set place in the ground, which is usually outdoors. When it rains, snows, or gets too hot, it makes practice unreasonable. To get around the problem of the traditional makiwara, I've constructed my own Rock & Roll style of makiwara called "the heavy-duty striking post."

The heavy-duty striking post lets you throw punches and kicks from many different angles, and you don't have to stay in a specific area to execute all of your strikes. You can circle the striking post and execute various types of strikes at any time without worrying about getting into the proper position.

MATERIALS

The construction of the striking post is fairly simple. For materials, you will need one 6-foot untreated telephone pole, 12 inches in diameter; a high-density foam pad, 2 × 4 feet; a piece of 18-ounce vinyl-coated nylon, 54 × 52-inches; a rubber tire approximately 52 inches in diameter and 6–8 inches in width; three to five 60-pound bags of premixed cement; three 4 × 1/2-inch lag screws; a 52 × 1/2-inch circle of plywood; and a few nails (see fig. 97).

97

CONSTRUCTION

Once you have all the materials, determine which side of the telephone pole will stand up; the thicker section should be on the bottom. Attach three 4 × 1/2-inch lag screws around the bottom of the post, staggering them approximately 8 inches apart, 3–4 inches from the very bottom. Screw the lag screws approximately 2 inches into the post (see fig. 98). These screws will prevent the post from moving once it is set in cement.

To prepare the tire to pour the cement into it, you must first cover the bottom of the tire with a round piece of 1/2-inch plywood that has the same diameter as the tire (see fig. 99). Nail the plywood to the bottom of the tire with 3–4-inch nails.

When the board is attached to the tire, bend any nails protruding inside the tire as much as possible so that the board will be secure when the cement is poured into it (see fig. 100).

Now lay the tire on the ground with the board on the bottom and place the telephone pole in the middle of the tire. Center the pole and pour three to five bags of wet mixed cement into the tire (see fig. 101). Tap the edges of the tire with a trowel to make sure the cement fills every space in the tire. Allow one or two days for the cement to dry.

100

101

Once the cement is dry, attach the high-density foam to the pole with duct tape. The height of the pad will depend on your height. The top height of my pad was approximately 5 feet 6 inches and I am 5 feet 9 inches (see fig. 102).

Take the piece of 18-ounce vinyl-coated nylon and lay it over the pad so that it extends approximately to 2–3 inches over the pad. Attach the top area of the vinyl with duct tape also (see fig. 103).

You will now need a heavy-duty (preferably electric) staple gun to secure the vinyl to the pole. Staple the top portion of the vinyl to the pole, stapling approximately 3–4 inches apart (see fig. 104). Because the telephone pole is so hard, you may have to pound the remainder of the staples into the post with a hammer. Staple the bottom portion of the vinyl around the pad all the way around the posts as you did with the top portion (see fig. 105).

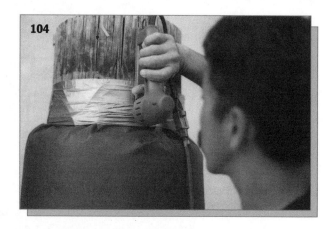

To make the striking post look neat, carefully apply a layer of duct tape around the circumference of the pole where the vinyl is stapled to the pole (see fig. 106). Once this is done, the heavy-duty striking post is ready to be used.

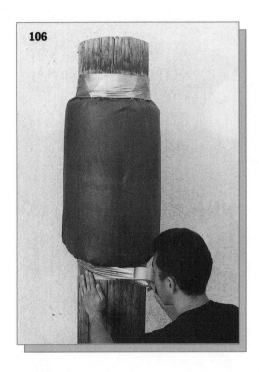

The weight of the heavy-duty striking post can be as much as 200–300 pounds, so make sure you have someone to help when moving the completed post.

I have used my post for many years and it shows no signs of wear and tear. It can be used indoors or outdoors and is an excellent tool for practicing full-power strikes and combinations.

TRAINING

The heavy-duty striking post can be used in a number of different ways. The post can be struck in the "traditional" Karate fashion, facing the post in the forward stance and striking it with a reverse punch for a set number of repetitions (see fig. 107).

You can also train the traditional front kick, side kick, and back kick in this way (see fig. 108). As you develop more power and accuracy, you will see the whole apparatus move when it is struck. This means that you are developing more power into your strikes.

The beauty of the heavy-duty striking post is most evident when striking the post at an unusual angle, such as with a roundhouse kick (see fig. 109), crescent kicks (see fig. 110), double kick (see fig. 111), Wing Chun punches (see fig. 112), palm strikes (see fig. 113), back fist (see fig. 114), or eye flicks (see fig. 115).

I have also used the heavy-duty striking post to practice "internal" system techniques. For Pa Kua, the post can be circled as one walks the Pa Kua circle, concentrating on the intricate Pa Kua footwork patterns (see fig. 116). As one gets closer to the post, the eight palm strikes can be employed on the pole in a random manner (see figs. 117–119). The pad allows the practitioner to strike the pole as hard as he or she would like without the fear of injuring the delicate structure of the open palm.

Tai Chi techniques can also be practiced on the heavy-duty striking post, as one can push the pole off-balance with Tai Chi's famous "grasp the swallow's tail" (see fig. 120), "diagonal flying" (see fig. 121), "grasp swallow's tail ward off" (see fig. 122), "brush knee and twist step" (see fig. 123), "fair lady works the shuttles" (see fig. 124), and other techniques.

The main principle I've employed when using the heavy-duty striking post for Tai Chi training is to root and hold a good base or stance and slowly press or push the top half of the post to push the pole off-balance slightly, uprooting the cement base.

Once you can do this comfortably and slowly, gradually increase the speed of the push until the push becomes a sudden jolt, to throw an opponent off-balance (see fig. 125). Remember that the base, depending on the tire size, can weigh up to 100-plus pounds. Adding to the weight of the pole, a heavy-duty striking post can weigh from 150 to 250 pounds. Pushing this pole around will definitely develop one's internal strength!

Even the five elements of Hsing-I can be practiced on the heavy-duty striking post. Splitting (*p'i-ch'uan,* see fig. 126), crushing (*peng-ch'uan,* see fig. 127), drilling (*tsuan-ch'uan,* see fig. 128), pounding (*pao ch'uan,* see fig. 129), and crossing (*heng-ch'uan,* see fig. 130) strikes can all be practiced on the heavy-duty striking post. When striking the pole, one should try to make the base of the post uproot slightly, to develop the "internal" drive, that make these strikes so effective.

I like the heavy-duty striking post for practicing specifically "internal" strikes because of the firm padding on the upper portion of the post. This prevents one's hand from getting injured or deformed while training, unlike a makiwara. Plus, the heavy-duty striking post "gives" when a lot of pressure is exerted on the pole, just like a real person, so the training is a little more realistic.

In reality, the heavy-duty striking post can be utilized for almost every striking system. I have used it to practice the flying side-kicks of Tae Kwon Do (see fig. 131), upside-down kicks of Capoeira (see fig. 132), elbow and knee strikes of Thai Boxing (see fig. 133), beginning and advanced techniques of boxing (see fig. 134), intricate hand strikes of Wing Chun (see fig. 135), and the deadly kicks of Savate (see fig. 136). As I have related, the training devices are limited only by your imagination!

131

132

CHAPTER 10

THE GROCERY BAG

During my years of studying many different kicking systems, I've always looked for tools and training devices that would improve my kicking performance. After years of searching for a portable, compact, easy-to-use, inexpensive training device, I found... the common, lightweight, plastic grocery bag.

The grocery bag offers a random target at varying distances, just like sparring. You can kick the bag as hard as you want and not be afraid of hurting yourself. Follow-through and snappy kicks can all be utilized on this bag. Almost every conceivable kick can be practiced on this bag without any ill effects to the kicker. From flying jump kicks to ground-level leg sweeps, the combinations are endless.

Another nice feature of the grocery bag is that you don't need a lot of room to use it, an eight by eight-foot square is about all you need to get a good kicking workout. But the best feature of the grocery bag is the cost—practically nothing, because you get them for free at the grocery store every time you buy groceries.

THE WORKOUT

To train your kicks using the grocery bag, put on some music, set your timer for three minutes, and start kicking at the grocery bag. The main objective at first is to keep the bag from touching the ground. Once you are comfortable with that exercise, try executing actual martial arts kicks to the bag, making sure the form and technique are good. Try to make the bag pop or snap while kicking it. You will eventually be able to tell when you hit the bag well, just by the sound of the bag being struck (see fig. 137).

As you get better, practice jumping kicks on the bag or any unusual kick you can think of that you may use on an opponent (see fig. 138). Remember, though, that the main objective of this drill is to prevent the bag from touching the ground.

Another interesting drill I utilize is to practice low kicks and sweeps to the bag for one round, trying to prevent the bag from going higher then waist level, and not letting the bag touch the ground. This drill develops control and accuracy of the devastating low kicks, but also accelerates your reaction time, because the bag will hit the ground sooner falling from waist level (see fig. 139).

I try to work at least three three-minute rounds with the grocery bag at the end of a workout. I like the freedom the bag offers because there's no resistance or hard pounding on your body, as there is with a heavy bag. I have used the grocery bag drills with my students many times, and they love it.

Another kicking drill that is good for improving one's stationary speed and accuracy for kicks is to hang the bag at eye level with a piece of string and to kick the bag as fast as possible without telegraphing the kick (see figs. 140–142). To further develop the speed and accuracy of kicks, cut the bag in half to limit the target size. When you execute the kick, it should be explosive and as fast as possible, to get the body used to the speed of a kick. You must also bring your leg back faster than you kicked it out, which improves the speed of the full execution of the kick.

Lastly, and most important, don't throw too many of these explosive speed kicks at one time. Limit yourself to ten repetitions of a specific kick to improve your speed and accuracy. If you practice too many of the speed and accuracy kicks, the kicks get sloppy and you will start to develop bad habits to compensate for muscle fatigue.

This speed and accuracy kicking drill can be applied to any kick at any level: high, medium, or low. To develop accuracy for follow-through kicks, again hang the bag at whatever level you choose with a piece of string see fig. 143).

To practice the full range of motion of a specific kick, this time use your whole body and follow through with the kick. The lightness of the bag lets your foot move through the intended target, letting you complete the full range of the kick. The best follow-through kicks to practice on this bag are the follow-through roundhouse kick (see figs. 144–146), the spinning back kick, crescent kicks, and even forward and backward ground-level sweeps.

Hand techniques can also be practiced in almost the same manner as the kicks. One can toss the bag in the air and practice a series of quick, snappy hand strikes, while also trying to prevent the bag from touching the ground. This drill will develop the quick movements for effective hand techniques and also the snap in one's hand strikes, if one snaps each strike executed onto the bag (see fig. 147). Doing this hand drill with the grocery bag for approximately three three-minute rounds will significantly improve the speed and snap in your hand technique.

To develop speed and accuracy in your hand strikes, the grocery bag can also be hung with a piece of string, at the head, stomach, or leg level, depending on the section of the body you would like to practice striking. Just as with the kicking drill for speed and accuracy, strike the hanging grocery bag with whatever hand strike you choose, as fast as possible, without tele-graphing your movement (see figs. 148–150). Doing the hand drill this way ensures the

accuracy of the hand strike and the explosive movement that it takes to execute the technique. Remember, only do approximately three sets of ten repetitions of each technique so as to ensure quality and proper form of each move.

If one wants to develop total body striking coordination, the grocery bag routine can be done with both hand and foot strikes. As with the previous drills, the grocery bag can be tossed in the air and struck with kicks and punches. Try to keep the bag floating without touching the ground for two or three three-minute rounds (see figs. 151–153).

The grocery bag can also be used to develop speed and accuracy for combination strikes of hands and feet, in the same manner described for punches and kicks. Simply hang the grocery bag at the desired height with a piece of string and practice a combination of hand and foot techniques on the suspended grocery bag (see figs. 154–158).

THE GROCERY BAG CHAMBER

A final drill I thoroughly enjoy is setting up a multiple hanging bag chamber. This involves hanging several grocery bags from strings, at different heights throughout one's training area. I like to hang at least six to ten bags and let them dangle from the ceiling (see fig. 159). Once this is done, I strike each bag with kicks for one three-minute round, with hand strikes for one three-minute round, and with a combination of hand and foot strikes for another five-minute round (see figs. 160–163).

This drill develops the feeling of being attacked by multiple opponents and the ability to react and judge random distances when striking at an attacker. One can also practice varying the techniques on each bag, so that one does not have to change the hanging height of the grocery bag every time one wants to practice a special technique.

This "bag chamber" drill is normally done for three three-minute rounds to get the full benefit of reacting to multiple opponents.

The uses of a grocery bag for martial arts training are endless. Probably a whole book could be done on its uses. Experiment with the above-listed drills, and you can realize the full training potential of the grocery training bag.

One student I have, who had a bad case of high blood pressure, did the grocery bag workout every day for one week and reduced his blood pressure enough so that he did not have to take high blood pressure medication again.

Try this grocery bag workout with your kicks, and you will see that you'll have your kicks in the "bag"!

CHAPTER 11

THE SMALL HANGING BAG

One of the most useful home training devices that practically every martial artist should have is a small hanging bag. A small hanging bag develops timing, distancing, and speed, and also helps condition your fists, elbows, feet, knees, and various striking areas. The small hanging bag is also inexpensive to make at home and easy to construct.

I have used the small hanging bag for almost every system that I have practiced. What I like about the small hanging bag is that it is not very heavy—unlike the heavy bag—yet it feels solid when struck and "gives" like a human body. The bag can be easily hung at different heights to focus on the strike that one is practicing. I have practiced almost every conceivable kick that I know, from Capoeira to Savate, on the small hanging bag, and the most exotic hand strikes from many esoteric systems that I've studied. The small hanging bag, when placed in the optimal position, makes practicing striking skills actually fun because of its unique "feel" when it is struck.

I have made many small hanging bags for many years and will share with you some of the secrets of its construction.

MATERIALS

The most important aspect in making a small hanging bag is selecting the material that the bag will be made of. I have experimented with various types of heavy cloth, heavy canvas, and even types of vinyl used in upholstery. I have found the best material to use to make a hanging bag is "Rip-Stop" vinyl, vinyl laminate, or vinyl-coated nylon. This special type of vinyl is used in making high-quality heavy bags and is also used as tarps to shield people from the sun. You can find this type of vinyl only at a vinyl specialty store, an upholstery shop, or maybe a canvas supply company that specializes in making canvas tarps and sails.

To see if the grade of "Rip-Stop" vinyl is good, I try to rip a small section of the vinyl using both hands. If I cannot rip it, the vinyl will be good for the construction of the small hanging bag. This is a special type of vinyl that is interlaced with fiberglass thread, which prevents the vinyl from being torn or ripped. The vinyl comes in many weights. The best weight for this bag is 18 ounces. So, when you go to a vinyl supply company, ask for the 18-ounce vinyl-coated nylon.

The best way to find the appropriate vinyl supply company is to look in the local Yellow Pages under upholstery supplies, vinyl supplies, or canvas manufacturing companies.

You will also need a one-inch metal ring to hang the small bag from, sand or gravel to fill the bag, and duct tape and nylon cord will also be needed to close and finish the bag. You can obtain these items at any hardware store (see fig. 164).

164

CONSTRUCTION

Once you have your "Rip-Stop" vinyl, cut a 36 × 16-inch piece (see fig. 165) then fold the piece in half so that you have a piece 18 × 16-inch (see fig. 166). The top of the bag will be where the two pieces of vinyl meet, and the bottom will be where the vinyl is folded. With a marking pen, outline a U shape along the edge of the vinyl with a one-inch border along the edges.

165

166

The top of the vinyl will be the top of the U, and the bottom will touch the bottom of the U (see fig. 167). Make sure the top of the U is left open so that you can later stuff the bag. Now mark another line along the edges of the U, half an inch from the edge (see fig. 168).

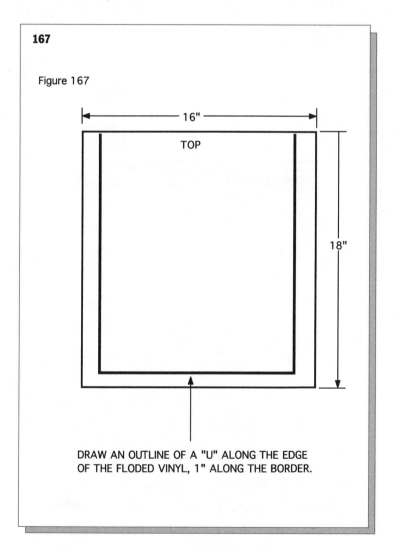

167

Figure 167

TOP

16"

18"

DRAW AN OUTLINE OF A "U" ALONG THE EDGE
OF THE FLODED VINYL, 1" ALONG THE BORDER.

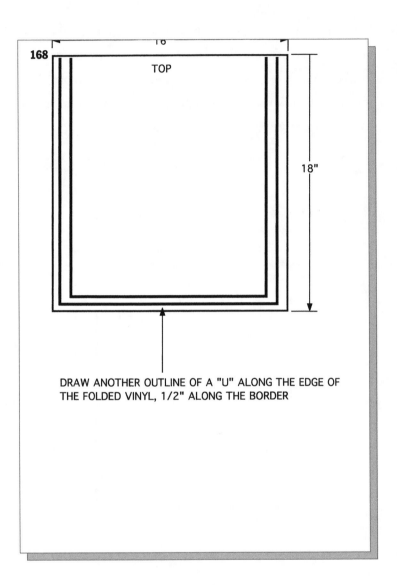

168

18"

TOP

DRAW ANOTHER OUTLINE OF A "U" ALONG THE EDGE OF
THE FOLDED VINYL, 1/2" ALONG THE BORDER

The next step is sewing the bag. Use a heavy-duty sewing
machine or an upholstery sewing machine to sew the vinyl
together. Sew the 1-inch border first (see fig. 169), then the

half-inch border (see fig. 170). Doubling the border gives more strength and life to the bag. Make sure you use a heavy nylon thread in the sewing machine. A cotton-fiber-based thread is weak and wears out quickly.

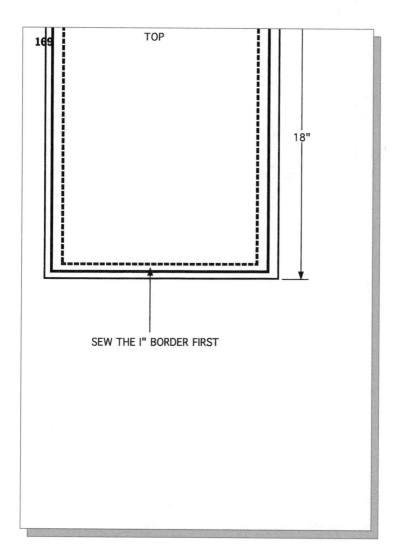

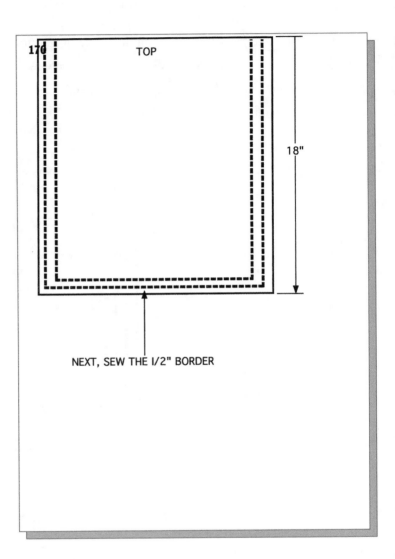

Once you have completed sewing the borders of the bag, put it aside and cut a 12 × 2-inch strip of "Rip-Stop" vinyl (see fig. 171). Fold the vinyl lengthwise so you have a 12 × 1-inch strip (see fig. 172). Sew the top or open edge together so that you now have a strap 12 × 1-inches (see fig. 173). Attach this strap to one side of the top edge of the small bag by sewing them together (see fig. 174) with the sewing machine.

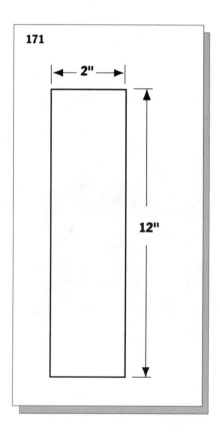

171

|← 2" →|

12"

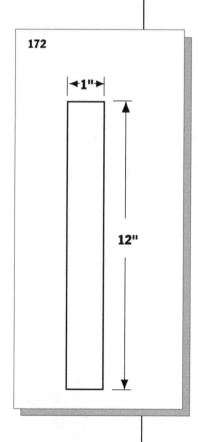

172

|←1"→|

12"

173

FIGURE 173

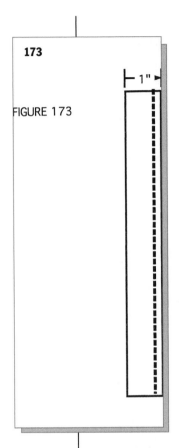

One end of the strap should be attached to the top edge of the bag. Once one end of the strap is attached to the bag, slip the strap through a metal ring one inch in diameter (see fig. 175). This ring will be used to hang the bag. Now attach the other end of the strap to the opposite top edge of the bag with the sewing machine. Make sure you

174

175

attach the strap no more than 2 inches from the top edge (see fig. 176).

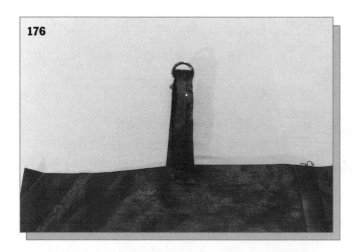

Turn the bag inside out, and you are now ready to stuff the bag. The bag can be stuffed with a variety of different materials: sand, cloth, beans, pebbles, etc., to fit your specific needs. For conditioning of the hands and feet I use sand. For accuracy, I fill the bag with cloth. For a normal bag, I usually stuff the bottom of the bag with rags (see fig. 177), the center of the bag with sand (see fig. 178), and the top

section of the bag with cloth (see fig. 179). This way the bottom of the bag will not be too hard to strike (eventually the bottom of the bag feels like cement, if there is no cloth to move and cushion the sand), and the top section filled with cloth prevents the sand from escaping from the top portion of the bag.

When the bag is stuffed and filled, hang it up at waist level (see fig. 180). You now must seal or close the bag so that the stuffing does not come out. Squeeze the unfilled neck portion of the bag with your hand and tape this section until you are sure that the stuffing will not come out (see fig. 181).

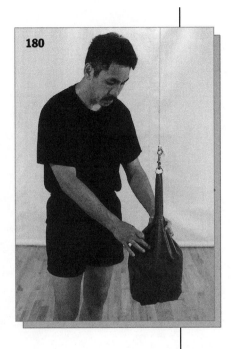

With some thick nylon cord, wrap and tie the section that has been taped until you cannot see the tape. Be neat while wrapping the cord around the top of the bag (see fig. 182). The small hanging bag is now completed.

When hanging the bag, I usually attach a 3/8-inch × 2-inch eye-hook to a large support beam in the ceiling. From the eyehook I hang an S hook and attach a 3/8-inch × 4-foot rope to it. I let the rope dangle from the eyehook to the level at which I would like to hang the bag. At the other end of the rope, I

attach a fastener clip (see fig. 183). The fastener clip allows me to take down the bag very easily when necessary.

182

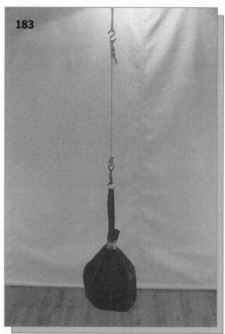

183

The more bags you make, the more confident you become in their construction. You can vary the size and shape of the bag to fit your own specific needs. I have many small hanging bags of different sizes, shapes, and weights, all for different purposes. I hang a few of my bags in a "chamber" at different heights, to give me the feel of multiple attackers (see fig. 184).

To practice in a "bag chamber," simply construct at least five to ten small hanging bags and place them in an appropriate area. A garage will sometimes do, or the branches of a large tree, but a special box made from one-inch pipe would be the best (see fig. 185).

Hang the bags at various heights, then start hitting them at random. As the bags get hit, they start to move and will actually hit you if you do not apply good footwork to evade them. This is an excellent drill to develop reaction, timing, and distancing for strikes.

I also use a single small hanging bag to develop "short energy" or the "one-inch" punch. Simply place your hand one inch away from the bag and strike the bag as hard as possible. When the "short energy" strike is developed, the bag will move 12–18 inches when struck with a short energy strike (see figs. 186–187).

Another unique technique that can be best practiced on the small hanging bag is the "hinge kick." Many martial arts systems don't have this kick, but this an excellent close-range kick if one has the flexibility. Stand in your fighting stance, no more than 18 inches from the bag (see fig. 188). With the lead leg, flip the outside edge of the foot toward the bag, striking the bag with the outer edge of your foot and little toe (see fig. 189). Unusual as this kick sounds and looks, it is very effective when used at close range (see fig. 190).

The headbutt can also be practiced on the small hanging bag. Because of the bag's size and compactness, striking the bag with one's head gives a realistic "feel" of actually headbutting an opponent. The small hanging bag should be hung at head level for practicing the forward, side, and rear headbutt. The headbutts should be practiced from a short range of no more than 6–8-inches, emphasizing a sudden snapping motion toward the middle of the bag (see figs. 191 and 192). Do not wind up or telegraph the butt, because your opponent will see the butt coming and move away from the strike.

To increase the impact of the blow, place your hand on the back of the bag and pull the bag toward your head as you strike the bag. A headbutt done in this fashion to an opponent's head is devastating (see figs. 193 and 194). Always remember to strike with the upper edge area of your head and to place your tongue on the roof of your mouth when delivering a headbutt.

The uppercut or upward angular strikes to the face can also be vigorously practiced on this bag, because of the special way the bag hangs at head level, which exposes it to a sharp upward angular strike that is normally hard to practice on a traditional heavy bag.

From the fighting stance, uppercuts (see fig. 195), upward palms (see fig. 196), flexed-wrist strikes (see fig. 197), and even focused front chin kicks (see fig. 198) can be practiced on the small hanging bag.

The uses and applications of small hanging bags are endless. I use it for Wing Chun strikes (see fig. 199), Tae Kwon Do kicks (see fig. 200), Escrima strikes (see fig. 201), and Thai Boxing elbows (see fig. 202), as well as for exotic, unusual striking methods (see fig. 203). The beauty of this training device is that it is so simple to build; no martial artist should be without it.

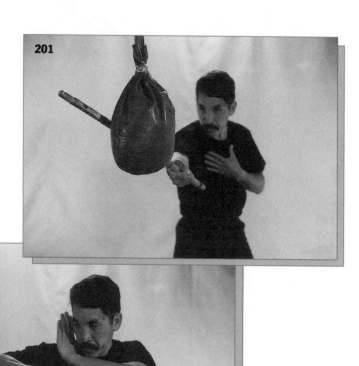

CHAPTER 12

THE CHOKING DUMMY

Over the past several years, interest in the grappling arts has boomed with the popularity of the "total" or "anything goes" types of martial arts competitions.

The public has noticed that the competitor who can apply a good choke on his opponent will usually win the overall competition. Practically every opponent in the early "total" or "anything goes" competitions was beaten by a choke hold. Because of the undeniable effectiveness of a good choke hold, I began earnestly studying the grappling arts, especially the art of Shimewaza, or strangling techniques.

I found that Judo and Ju-Jitsu practitioners had the most knowledge of this art because many of the deadly strangleholds were frequently applied in open competition.

After years of experimentation, often using myself as a guinea pig and getting "choked out," or forced to submit by means of a choke, by experienced Judokas and Ju-Jitsu stylists, I've learned the two basic principles of an effective choke: stop the blood supply to the brain or stop the air supply to the brain.

Of these two basic principles, I have found that stopping the blood supply to the brain by blocking the carotid arteries is the most effective and efficient method to defeat an opponent. The beauty of a carotid choke is that many times an opponent doesn't feel that he is in any danger while the choke is being applied. Then, in a few short seconds, the light goes out and the opponent is rendered unconscious. One immediately applies *katsu* or *kappo* (resuscitation techniques) to one's opponent.

When a choke cuts off the air supply, the opponent feels a sense of panic and thrashes about violently, oftentimes shaking off the would-be choker. A person has remarkable strength when he or she feels a sense of panic.

As mentioned in the discussion of the previous choke (cutting off the air supply), an opponent who feels pain in his or her neck will violently resist, doing anything to get loose. Even if it means poking your eyes or smashing against the wall, your opponent will do it to get away.

To practice applying an effective choke, I knew I had to create a device that would have the right "feel." I realized that I would have to make a training tool that would allow all the intricate subtlety that would make a choke effective. I needed to create this device for several reasons, but the most important reason was that after you practice choking techniques for awhile, you run out of training partners who are willing to be "choked out."

After years of trial and error and countless hours of experimentation, I finally came up with a training device that has definitely enhanced my ability to apply an effective carotid choke as well as an air-obstructing choke. I now affectionately refer to this training device as "the choking dummy." The choking dummy that I created gives you the proper feel—the proper hand and arm positions to apply an appropriate choke.

The beauty of this device is that you can practice a specific choke over and over without fear of injuring your partner. The choking dummy is also a willing partner, whereas before the choking dummy, I always had to practice choking techniques on a live, and oftentimes reluctant, partner.

MATERIALS

To make this device it requires a little patience and practice. After a few practice sessions, you will be able to create a realistic and practical choking dummy.

All you need is a thin piece of carpet approximately 66 × 34 inches (use a thin weave of carpet, not thick shag-rug style), a roll of 2-inch duct tape, another roll of one-inch masking tape, and some newspaper (see fig. 204). You may find the piece of carpet in a scrap or remnant pile at a well-stocked carpet store.

CONSTRUCTION

First, take the piece of carpet and roll it tight, width-wise, so you have a rolled piece of carpet approximately 34 × 5 inches in diameter (see fig. 205). The circumference of the rolled piece of carpet should be 14–15 inches, the average size of a normal person's neck.

Next, secure the carpet so that it doesn't unravel by taping both ends of the carpet roll with duct tape around the circumference of the carpet roll. Also tape the middle of the carpet roll so that the roll is firm and secure (see fig. 206).

Now comes the tricky part, the shaping of the head. This section may take some practice, so don't be discouraged if the head does not come out right the first time. First crumple a lot of newspaper and form a large ball, about the size of the back of your head, and secure this ball of newspaper with masking tape to the end of one side of the carpet roll. Shape the ball until it looks like the back of a head by squeezing and pressing the newspaper wad to the appropriate shape (see fig. 207). Then place another wad of newspaper on the top of the head area and secure it with masking tape. Use your head as a model, and shape the top of the head

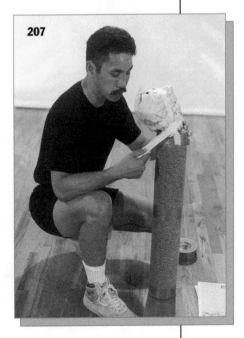

area by pressing and squeezing the crumpled newspaper into the proper position.

Next is the trickiest area, the front of the head. Crumple more newspaper, place it in the front of the head area, and secure it with masking tape (see fig. 208). With your thumbs, press into the crumpled newspaper approximately where the eye sockets would be. Tape this section over with masking tape so that the indentations left by your thumbs will remain in the crumpled newspaper (see fig. 209).

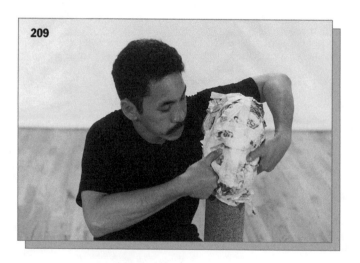

Just below and between the eye sockets will be the nose area. Crumple a small piece of newspaper into a ball approximately 3 inches in diameter and place it below and between the eye sockets, as if it were a nose. Secure the nose with masking tape, shaping it with your fingers by pressing and squeezing the crumpled newspaper (see fig. 210).

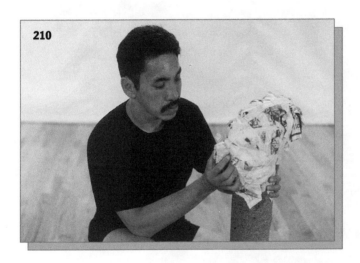

210

For the area just below the nose, crumple a large 5 × 8-inch section of newspaper, which will now be the mouth, chin, and jaw area. Place this piece of newspaper below the nose area and secure it with the masking tape (see fig. 211). Add smaller crumpled balls of newspaper along the jaw line of the dummy's head to form a distinct jaw line, which is crucial to the effectiveness of the dummy (see fig. 212). Add another small ball of crumpled newspaper to the dummy's chin area and secure it with masking tape (see fig. 213).

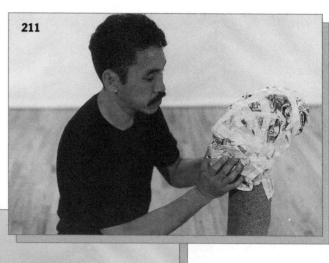

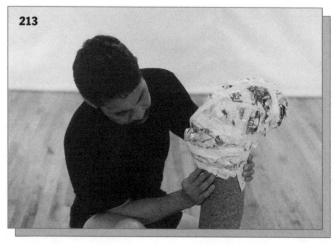

Press an indentation where the mouth area should be, and tape this area over with masking tape (see fig. 214). Now look at the dummy's head and see which sections it lacks or has too much of. Use your head as a model. Add or subtract the newspaper accordingly.

214

Once you have the rough shape of the dummy's head, you are ready to put on the finishing touches. Slowly and deliberately apply the "facial skin" to the dummy with duct tape.

The duct tape should be applied in long deliberate strips, going around the circumference of the head, starting at the neck area, in a horizontal pattern (see fig. 215). At each 1 1/2-inch interval, apply another strip of duct tape until you get to the temple area of the head. Place 14-inch-long strips of duct tape over the crown area of the head until it is completely covered (see fig. 216).

Press and push the key features to shape them into the proper shape of a real person, and secure the area with duct tape. Remember that the key areas are the eyes, nose, and—most important for the choke—the jaw and chin area.

Once you have touched up your dummy with the duct tape so that it has nice smooth skin, you should be ready to practice full-power chokes!

You will find that, through using this dummy, you will develop the sensitivity of the fine art of Shimewaza.

Ask a good Judoka to refine your technique on the choking dummy, because many fine pointers can be developed using the dummy to make your choking techniques more effective. I have been using this dummy now for years and have had remarkable success at applying a choke when grappling with live opponents. I can truthfully say that this dummy has been responsible for hundreds of submissions.

The standard rear choke can be practiced over and over with either arm, simply by getting behind the dummy and encircling the dummy's neck with the biceps and the forearm (see fig. 217) and squeezing on the sides of the dummy's neck where the carotid arteries (see fig. 218) would be, using the opposite hand to accentuate the choke (see fig. 219). Be sure to switch from left to right arm to practice a smooth transition when applying the standard carotid choke (see fig. 220).

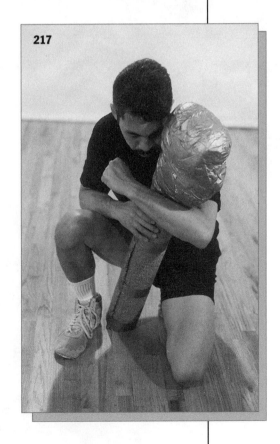

217

The quicker one can slide the forearm and squeeze the imaginary carotid arteries, the more efficient the choke. One can also apply a quick leg squeeze to the dummy's body to soften the opponent up (see fig. 221), but be careful not to leave your leg there too long—if the opponent knows his leg locks, he can apply a crippling counter (see figs. 222–224).

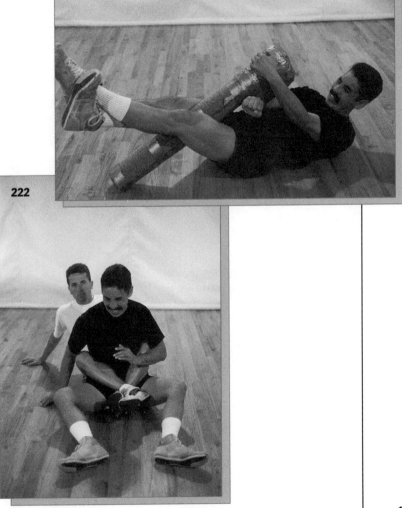

Squeezing the dummy's body is a great way to practice the fabled "guard" position (see fig. 225) of Ju-Jitsu. By squeezing the body of the dummy for 10 to 30 seconds at a time, you will develop the specialized adductor muscles used to hold a good "guard" position.

225

Another great choke to practice is what is sometimes called the "lock choke," or a "chancery" in law enforcement circles. Simply encircle the dummy's neck with your forearm, making sure that the chin of the dummy is directly over the bend of your elbow (see fig. 226). With the same arm, place your hand into the fold of

226

your opposite elbow joint (see fig. 227). Place your free hand
behind the back of the dummy's head, cupping it (see fig. 228).
Squeeze the encircling forearm tight around the dummy's neck
and push your head firmly into the back of the dummy's head,
which accentuates the choke (see fig. 229). This choke should
be practiced over and over, switching from one encircling arm
to the other until it can be done unconsciously, just by tactile
sense. Try doing this drill blindfolded (see fig. 230).

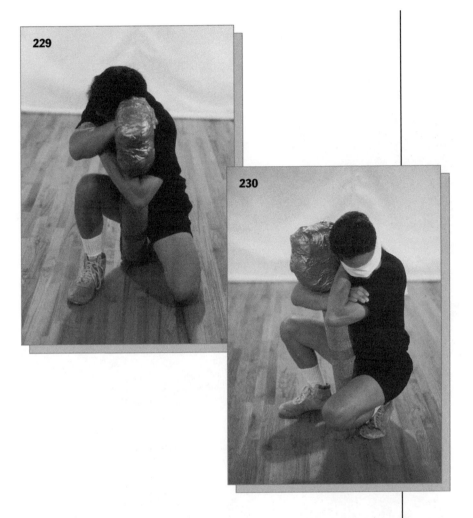

Forward chokes can also be practiced on the choking dummy from many different angles. A standard forward choke that can be practiced involves having the face of the dummy positioned toward your body (see fig. 231). With one arm, encircle the back of the dummy's neck area, placing your elbow directly behind the base of the skull area (see fig. 232) as you bring the same hand around to your opposite shoulder (see fig. 233).

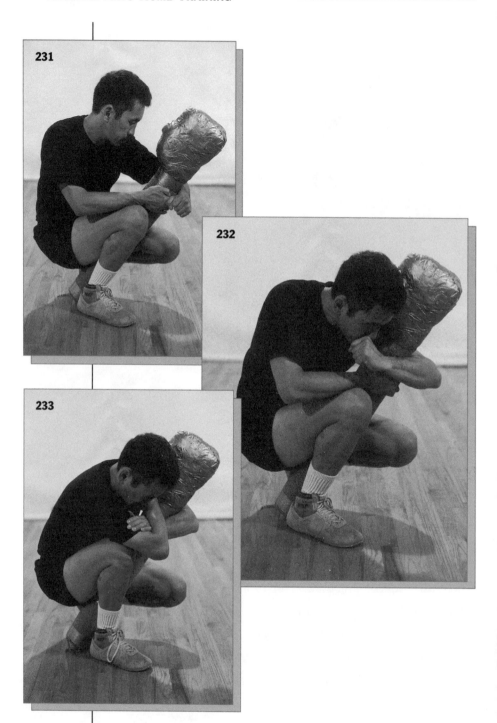

Your other hand/forearm should be placed on the opposite shoulder (see fig. 234), with the forearm pressing against the other carotid artery (see fig. 235). Squeeze your forearms together and press the dummy's head to one side to increase the effectiveness of the choke (see fig. 236).

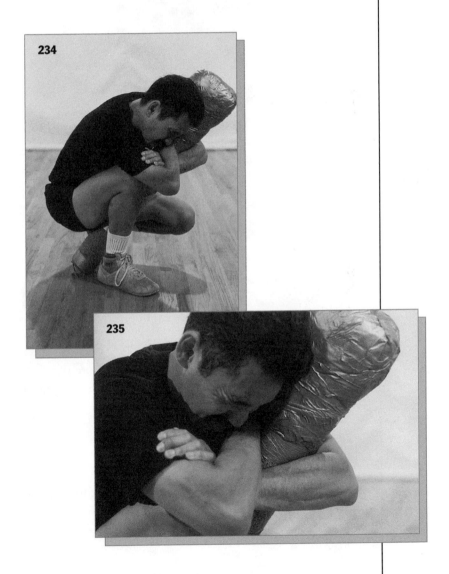

234

235

This choke, as with all the chokes, should eventually be practiced blindfolded to increase the intricate tactile sensitivity that is involved in executing an effective choke.

One of my favorite chokes to practice on the choking dummy is the guillotine choke. I have used this choke thousands of times on opponents who have tried to tackle me from the front, hoping to knock me down and finish me off.

The choking dummy has been responsible for my perfecting this frontal choke. To practice the guillotine choke on the choking dummy, lean the choking dummy on your chest or stomach while kneeling, at approximately a

45-degree angle to the ground. The dummy's face should be facing your body (see fig. 237). Quickly bring one forearm under the chin of the dummy and plant it into the throat area of the dummy (see fig. 238). Place this same hand into the fold of the opposite elbow and place your other hand firmly into the back of the neck area of the choking dummy, forming a figure 4 lock with the neck and the forearms (see fig. 239). Pull up on the forearm to the throat and push down on the top of the head area of the choking dummy with your chest, which will simulate cutting off the air to the opponent's lungs (see fig. 240).

This choke should be practiced until you can smoothly alternate forearms to the throat and locking the choke in. Eventually do this choke blindfolded when you are comfortable with it. There are literally countless chokes that one can practice with the choking dummy. This chapter is merely a guide to point you in the right direction, to understanding the concepts of a choke and then applying it to a training apparatus.

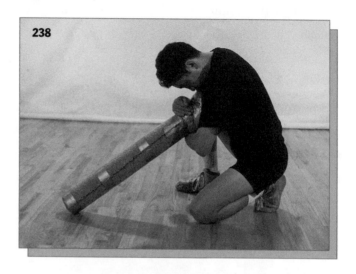

I have choked out countless people in a variety of ways by first practicing the techniques on the choking dummy (don't forget, I have also been choked out countless times!). Remember the principles of cutting off the airway or blood supply.

Some unusual chokes have included leg chokes (see fig. 241), forearm leg chokes (see fig. 242), knuckle chokes (see fig. 243), and foot chokes (see fig. 244). And there are countless variations.

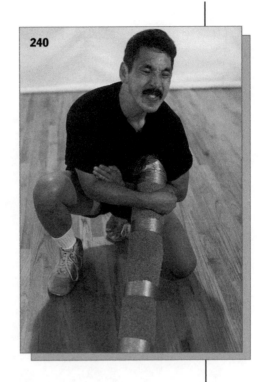

Try building your own choking dummy, and you'll find that your grappling opponent will be all "choked up" over your prowess!

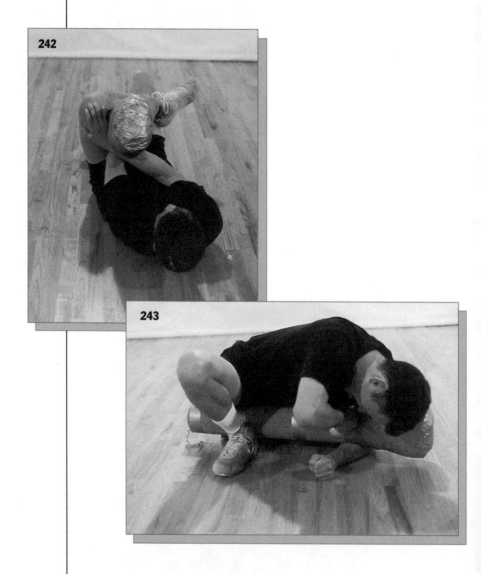

242

243

244

Conclusion

The secret of success is constancy to purpose.

—Benjamin Disraeli

As one can see after reading this book, building and training with one's own custom-made home training equipment can be easy, fun, and economical, if one doesn't limit oneself to "normal" or "conventional" methods of training. As I have mentioned throughout this book, creating, building, and using one's own personal home training equipment is only limited by one's imagination and creativity!

Imagine how dull the martial arts world would be if we only trained one way all the time. *Vive la différence!*

Diversification, variety, and change are the spice of life! It is because of these qualities that we now have such a rich martial arts culture. Therefore, take a step out of the traditional training methods and try building one of the devices in this book and using your own personal martial arts training routine. Remember, my training methods should act only as a guide—you should adapt the equipment to fit your specific needs. Eventually, I hope you will build your own unique home training devices and methods and share the information with the world!

Good luck on your own personal Quest for the Best.

Keep on Rocking & Rolling!

—Mike Young

About the Author

Mike Young has spent the last thirty years training in a wide array of martial arts disciplines, and has drawn from them all in developing his own style of full contact fighting. Mike has traveled the world, including such places as mainland China, Taiwan, Hong Kong, Brazil, Indonesia, Hawaii, France, and Belgium, to train in martial arts and is also a certified Police Defensive Tactics instructor. In addition to serving as a law enforcement officer, boxing coach, and martial arts instructor, Mike has been a contributing editor for a major international martial arts magazine for the past twelve years.

Among the styles Mike Young has studied and drawn from are Aikido, Boxing, Capoeira, Chinese Wrestling, Doce Pares Escrima, Eagle Claw Kung Fu, Hapkido, Hsing I, Jeet Kune Do, Judo, Jujitsu, Kajukenbo, Kali, Karate, Kenpo Karate, Krav Maga, Lua, Monkey Kung Fu, Northern Praying Mantis

Kung Fu, Northern Shaolin Kung Fu, Savate, Shootwrestling, Taekwondo, Tai Chi Chuan, Taido, Thai Boxing, Western Wrestling, and Wing Chun Kung Fu. Through his travels and wide training experience, he has developed many unique training methods and modified and updated many traditional methods for modern conditions. Some of these methods are shared with you in *Martial Arts Home Training*.

The author with the famous "Monkey King," Master Lia Wu Ch'ang, in Keelung, Taiwan, 1992.